2011 TOP ROCK HITS
FOR GUITAR

Produced by
Alfred Music Publishing Co., Inc.
P.O. Box 10003
Van Nuys, CA 91410-0003
alfred.com

Printed in USA.

ISBN-10: 0-7390-8313-9
ISBN-13: 978-0-7390-8313-0

Crowd photo: © iStockphoto.com / Milan Klusacek

CONTENTS

1983

Words and Music by
TIM PAGNOTTA, TYLER GLENN, BRANDEN CAMPBELL,
ELAINE DOTY and CHRISTOPHER ALLEN

Moderately fast ♩ = 152

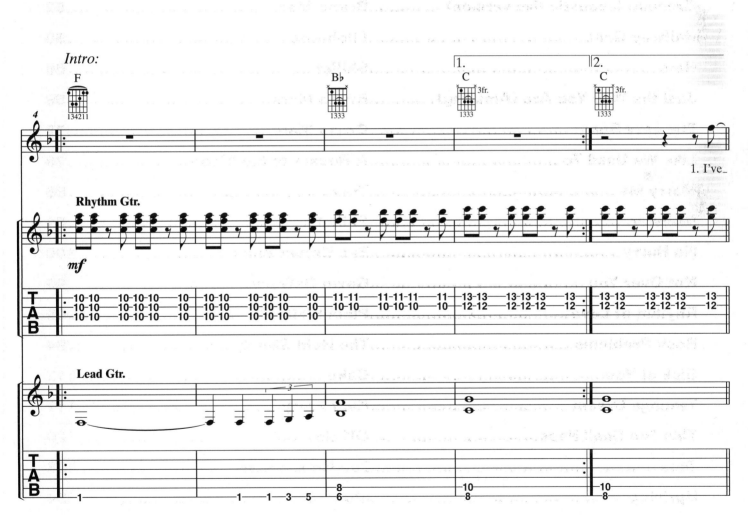

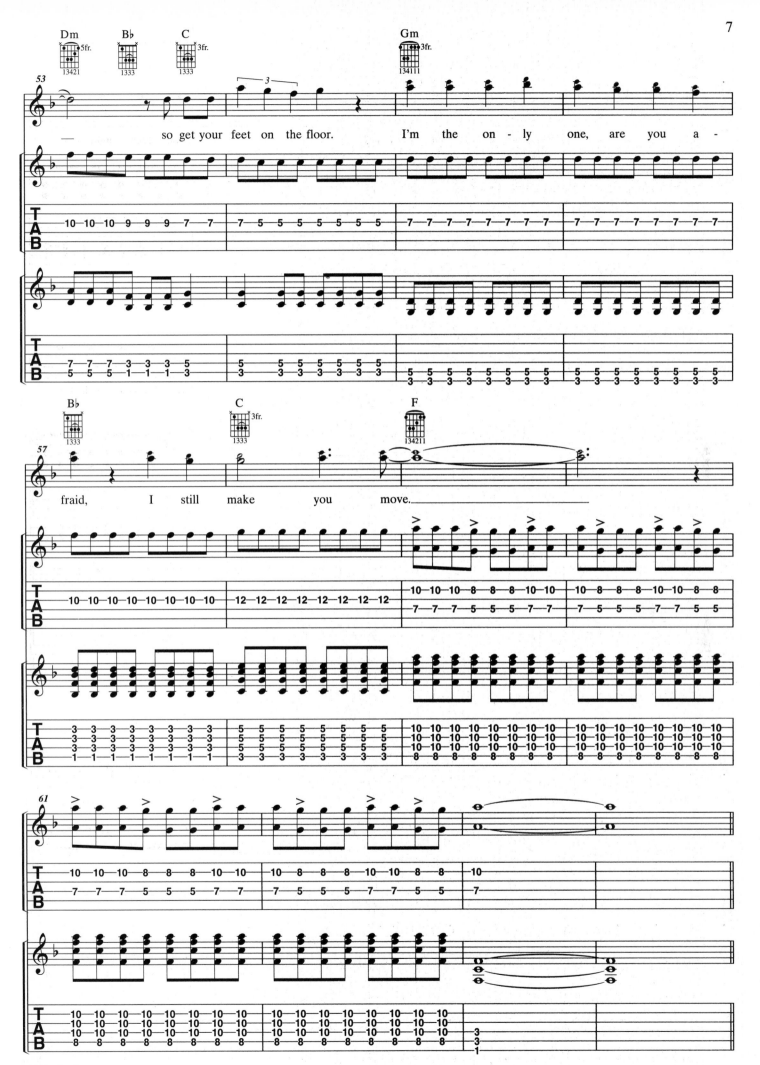

so get your feet on the floor. I'm the on - ly one, are you a -

fraid, I still make you move.

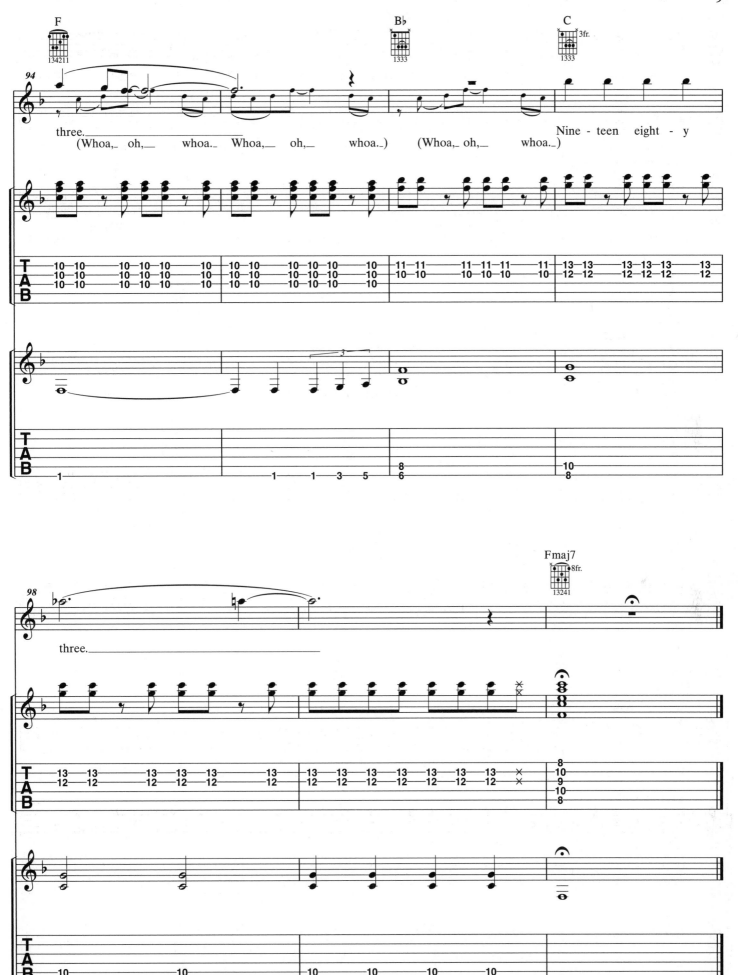

ANIMAL

Words and Music by
TIM PAGNOTTA, TYLER GLENN, BRANDEN CAMPBELL,
ELAINE DOTY and CHRISTOPHER ALLEN

Here we go a-gain.___ I kind-a wan-na be more than friends,___ so take it eas-y on me.

12

Animal - 6 - 3

Animal - 6 - 4

Bridge:

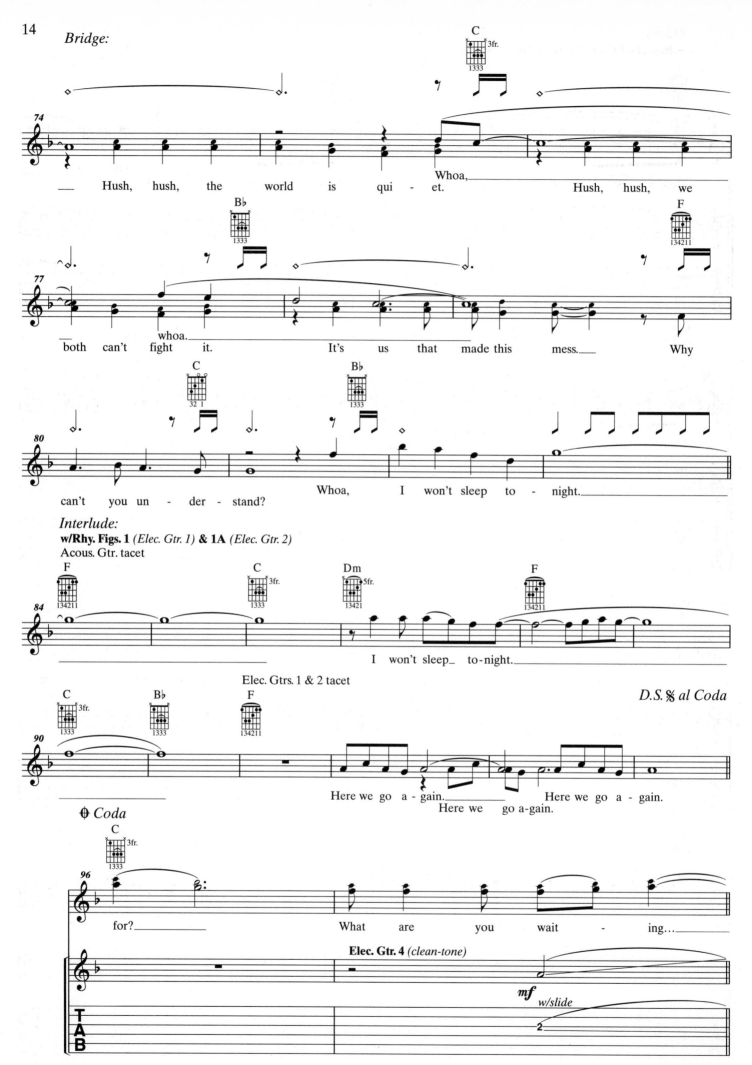

Hush, hush, the world is qui - et. Whoa,_____ Hush, hush, we

both can't fight it. It's us that made this mess.___ Why

can't you un - der - stand? Whoa, I won't sleep to - night.___

Interlude:
w/Rhy. Figs. 1 *(Elec. Gtr. 1)* **& 1A** *(Elec. Gtr. 2)*
Acous. Gtr. tacet

I won't sleep_ to-night.___

Elec. Gtrs. 1 & 2 tacet

D.S. %- al Coda

Here we go a - gain.___ Here we go a - gain.
Here we go a-gain.

Coda

for?___ What are you wait - ing...___

Elec. Gtr. 4 *(clean-tone)*

mf
w/slide

AWAKE AND ALIVE

All gtrs. in Drop D: ⑥ = D

Moderately ♩ = 84

Words and Music by
JOHN COOPER and BRIAN HOWES

Chorus:

Bridge:

Chorus:

Elec. Gtr. 3 resume chorus fig. simile

wake, I'm a - live, now I___ know what I___ be - lieve in - side.

BURN

*All gtrs. in Drop D, down 1 whole step:
⑥ = C   ③ = F
⑤ = G   ② = A
④ = C   ① = D

Words and Music by
TOBIN ESPERANCE, JERRY HORTON,
JACOBY SHADDIX and ROBERT HUFF

Moderately ♩ = 94

Intro:

Rhy. Fig. 1
Elec. Gtr. 1 *(w/dist.)*

*Recording sounds one whole step lower than written.
**Chords are implied.

end Rhy. Fig. 1

w/Rhy. Fig. 1 *(Elec. Gtr. 1)*

I did-n't know you were a_____ fake, ev-'ry lie straight to my____ face.

So blind I could not see right be-hind my back you stabbed me.

Verse:

w/Rhy. Fig. 1 *(Elec. Gtr. 1)* 2 times, simile

1. I should've known you were a_____ bitch, shut up, you're mak-ing me_____ sick.
2. You turn me in-side____ out, my world is up-side____ down.

Elec. Gtr. 2 *(w/dist.)*

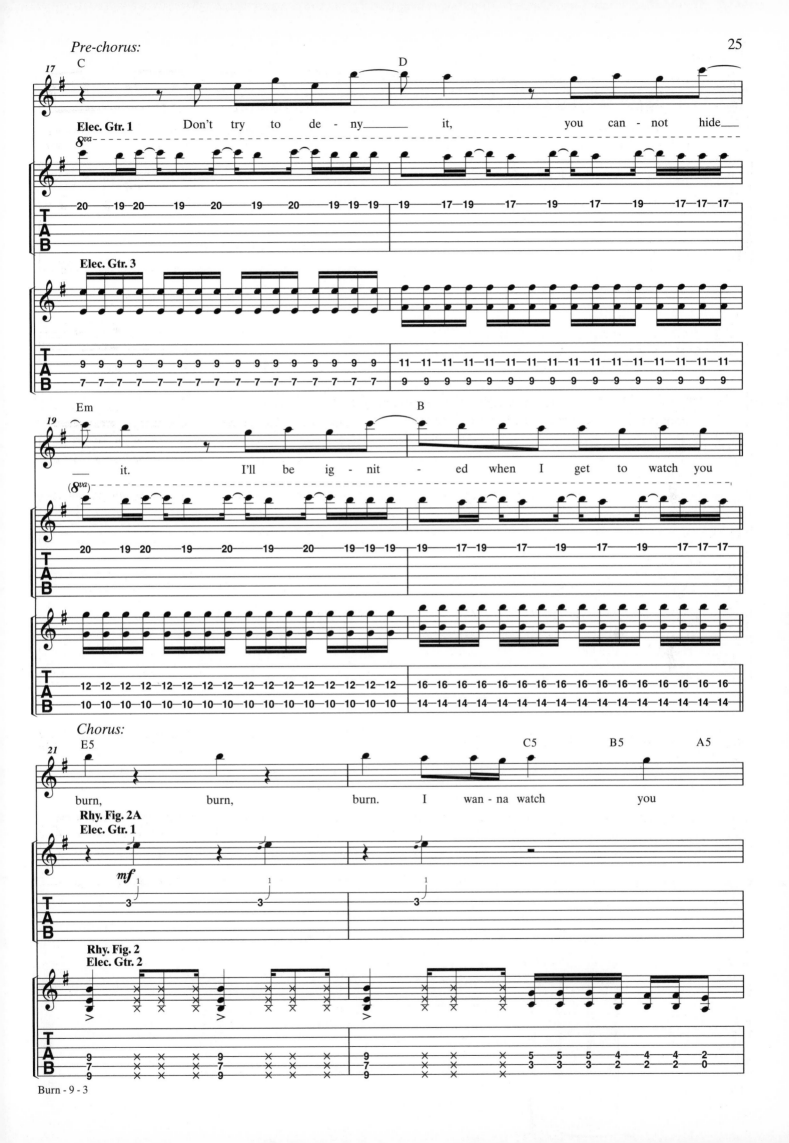

26

Burn - 9 - 4

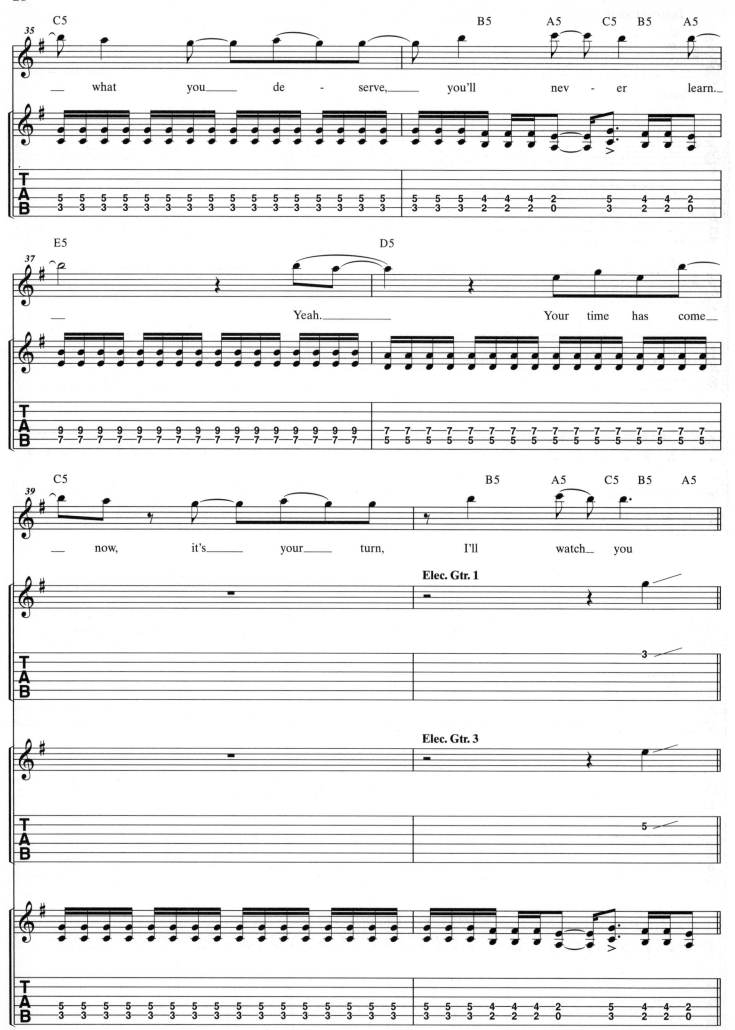

Instrumental:

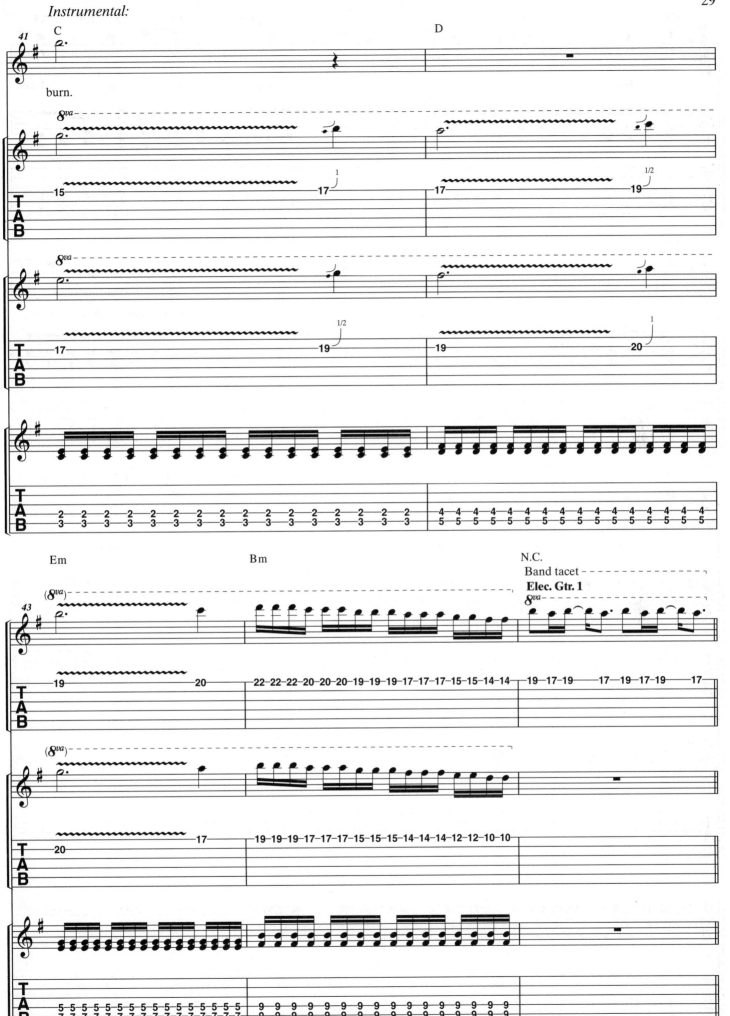

Chorus:

CALIFORNIA GURLS

Words and Music by
KATY PERRY, LUKASZ GOTTWALD,
MAX MARTIN, BONNIE MCKEE,
BENNY BLANCO and CALVIN BROADUS

California Gurls - 3 - 2

Snoop rap:
Toned, tan, fit and ready.
Turn it up 'cause it's getting heavy.
Wild, wild West Coast, these are the girls I love the most.
I mean the ones, I mean, like she's the one.
Kiss her, touch her, squeeze her buns.

The girl's a freak, she drive a Jeep, and live on the beach.
I'm okay, I won't play.
I love the bait, just like I love LA.
Venice Beach and Palm Springs, summertime is everything.

Homeboys bangin' out.
All that a** hangin' out.
Bikinis, zucchinis, martinis,
No weenies, just a king and a queenie.
Katy, my lady. (Yeah.)
Lookie here, baby. I'm all up on ya,
'Cause you're representin' California.
(To Chorus:)

COUNTRY BOY

Words and Music by
AARON LEWIS

Country Boy - 5 - 1

Chorus:

COUSINS

Lyrics by
EZRA KOENIG
Music by
CHRIS BAIO, ROSTAM BATMANGLIJ,
EZRA KOENIG and CHRISTOPHER TOMSON

Cousins - 5 - 1

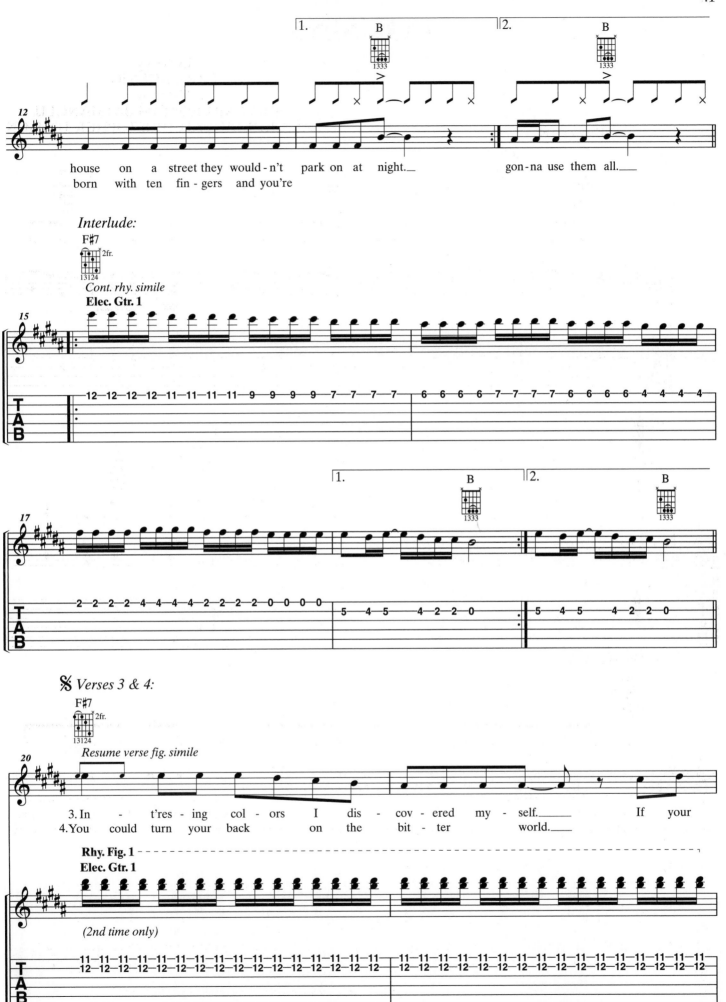

house on a street they would-n't park on at night.__ gon-na use them all.__
born with ten fin - gers and you're

Interlude:

Cont. rhy. simile
Elec. Gtr. 1

Verses 3 & 4:

Resume verse fig. simile

3. In - t'res - ing col - ors I dis - cov - ered my - self.____ If your
4. You could turn your back on the bit - ter world.___

Rhy. Fig. 1
Elec. Gtr. 1

(2nd time only)

FIREWORK

Words and Music by
KATY PERRY, MIKKEL ERIKSEN,
TOR ERIK HERMANSEN,
SANDY WILHELM and ESTER DEAN

Firework - 3 - 1

FORGET YOU

Words and Music by
CHRISTOPHER BROWN, PETER HERNANDEZ,
ARI LEVINE, PHILIP LAWRENCE
and THOMAS "CEE LO" CALLAWAY

Forget You - 4 - 1

GRENADE
(acoustic live version)

Words and Music by
CLAUDE KELLY, PETER HERNANDEZ, BRODY BROWN,
PHILIP LAWRENCE, ARI LEVINE and ANDREW WYATT

1. Eas - y come, eas - y go, that's just how you live. Oh, take, take, take it all,
2. Black, black, black and blue, beat me 'til I'm numb. Tell the dev - il I said "Hey" when you get

but you nev - er give. Should - 've known you was trou - ble from the first kiss, had your
back to where you're from. Mad wom - an, bad wom - an, that's just what you are. Yeah, you'll

Grenade - 4 - 1

HALFWAY GONE

Words and Music by
JASON WADE, KEVIN RUDOLF,
JUDE COLE and JACOB KASHER

Halfway Gone - 4 - 1

57

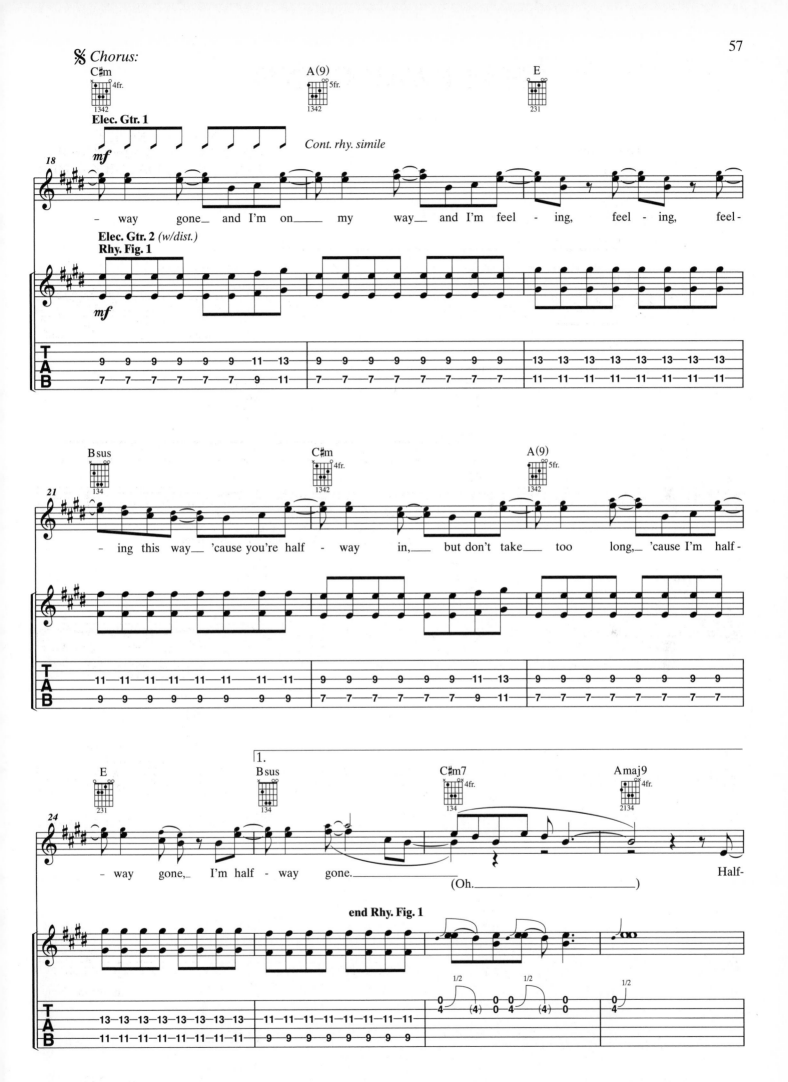

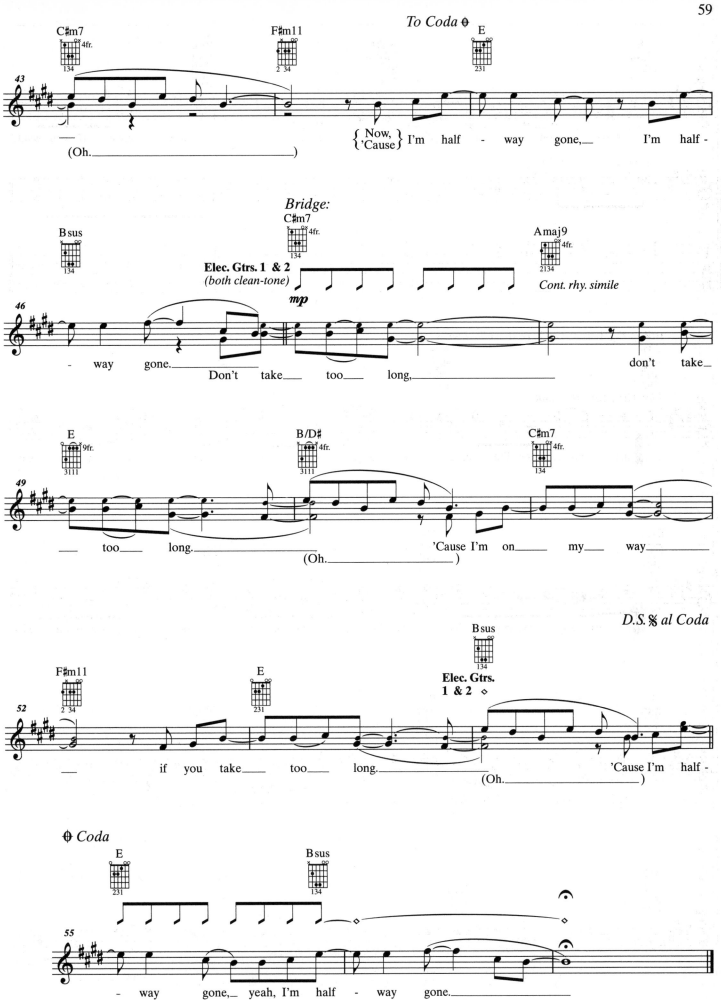

HERO

*All gtrs. in Drop D, down 1/2 step:

⑥ = D♭ ③ = G♭
⑤ = A♭ ②ﾞ = B♭
④ = D♭ ① = E♭

Words and Music by
JOHN COOPER and KOREY COOPER

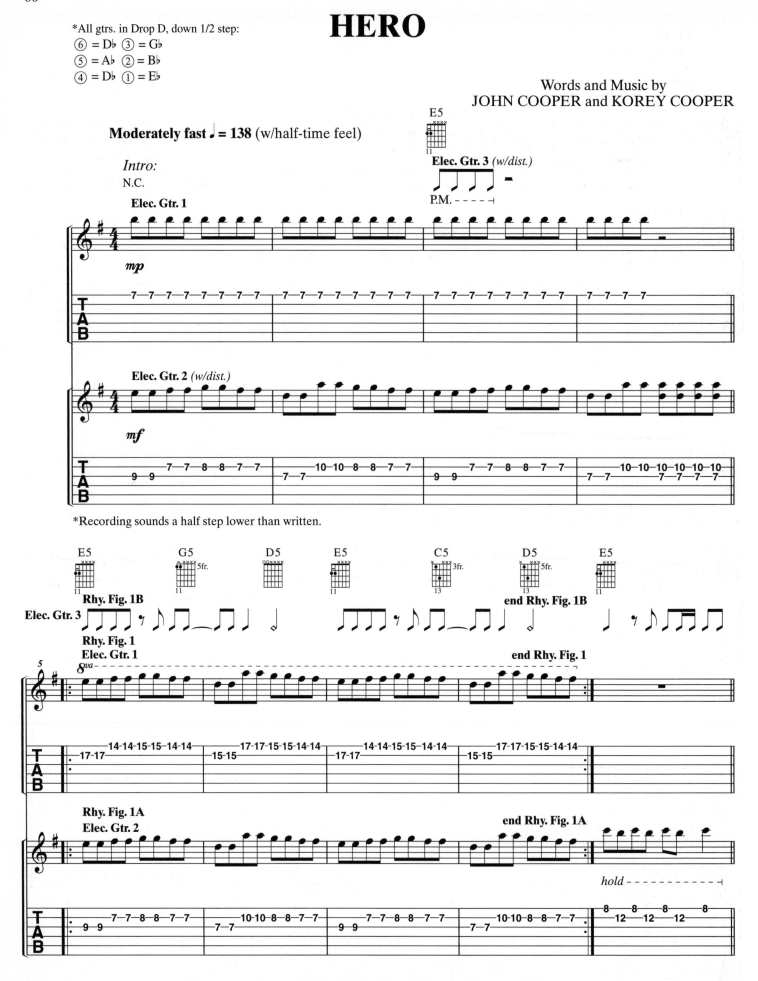

*Recording sounds a half step lower than written.

Hero - 8 - 1

Verse:

Elec. Gtrs. 1 & 2 tacet

*Cue-size notes 2nd time only.

62

Chorus:
w/Rhy. Figs. 1 *(Elec. Gtr. 1),* **1A** *(Elec. Gtr. 2),* **& 1B** *(Elec. Gtr. 3), each 2 times*

66

67

JUST THE WAY YOU ARE (AMAZING)

Words and Music by
KHALIL WALTON, PETER HERNANDEZ,
PHILIP LAWRENCE, ARI LEVINE
and KHARI CAIN

Just the Way You Are (Amazing) - 4- 1

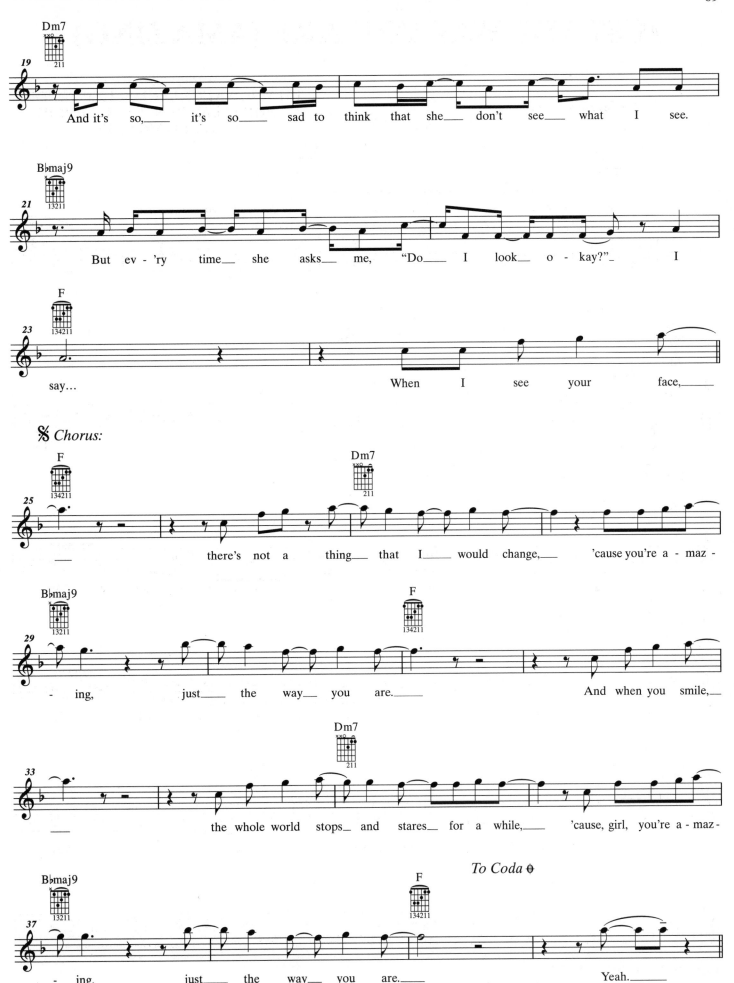

Verse 2:

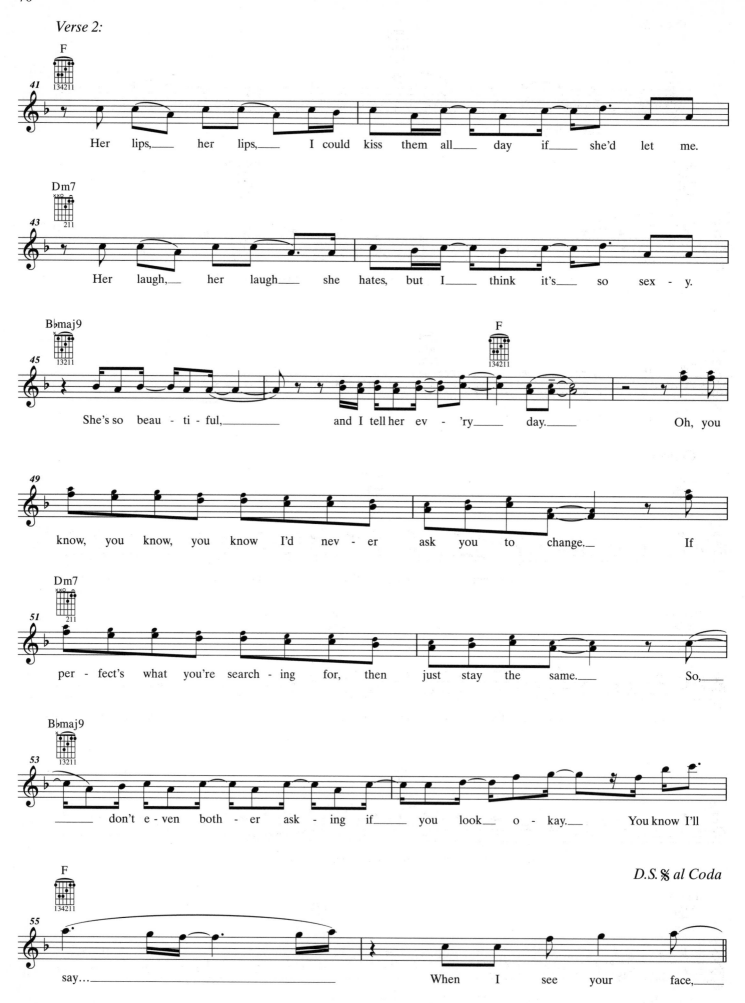

THE LAZY SONG

Words and Music by
PETER HERNANDEZ, PHILIP LAWRENCE,
ARI LEVINE and KEINAN WARSAME

Moderately slow reggae feel ♩ = 88

Chorus:

To - day, I don't feel like do - ing an - y - thing. *(Whistled)*

I just wan - na lay in my bed.___ *(Whistled)* Don't

feel like pick - ing up___ my phone,___ so leave a mes - sage at___ the tone,___ 'cause to -

day, I swear I'm not do - ing an - y - thing. Uh, 1. I'm gon - na

Verse:

kick my feet up, then stare at the fan,___ turn the T V on, throw my hand in my pants.
(2.) I'll wake up, do some P - nine - ty - X, meet a real - ly nice girl, have some real - ly nice sex. And

LIKE WE USED TO

Words and Music by
NICK SANTINO, JUSTIN RICHARDS, ERIC HALVORSEN,
ANDREW COOK, DAN YOUNG and LOREN BRINTON

Like We Used To - 5 - 1

Chorus:

MONSTER

*All gtrs. in Drop D, down 1 whole step:
⑥ = C ③ = F
⑤ = G ② = A
④ = C ① = D

Words and Music by
JOHN COOPER and GAVIN BROWN

Moderately fast ♩ = 132

Intro:

Rhy. Fig. 1
**Elec. Gtr. 1 (w/dist.)

end Rhy. Fig. 1

*Recording sounds a whole step lower than written.
**Elec. Gtr. 1 dbld. 2nd time.

Verse 1:
w/Rhy. Fig. 1 (Elec. Gtr. 1) 2 times

The se-cret side of me, I nev-er let you see. I keep it caged_ but I can't con-trol it.

So stay a-way from me, the beast is ug-ly, I feel the rage_ and I just can't hold it.

Verses 2 & 3:
w/Rhy. Fig. 1 (Elec. Gtr. 1)

2. It's scratch-ing on the walls, in the clos-et, in the halls. It comes a-wake_ and I
3. My se-cret side I keep hid un-der lock and key. I keep it caged_ but I

can't con-trol it. Hid-ing un-der the bed, in my bod-y, in my head. }
can't con-trol it. 'Cause, if I let him out, he'll tear me up, break me down. }

Elec. Gtr. 1

Monster - 5 - 1

MARRY ME

Words and Music by
SAM HOLLANDER and PAT MONAHAN

Marry Me - 4 - 1

NOT OVER YOU

Words and Music by
GAVIN DEGRAW and RYAN TEDDER

*Recording sounds a half step higher than written.
Chord frames and TAB numbers relative to capo.
**Suggested strum pattern.

ROCK PROBLEMS

Words and Music by
CRAIG FINN, TAD KUBLER
and JOHN REIS

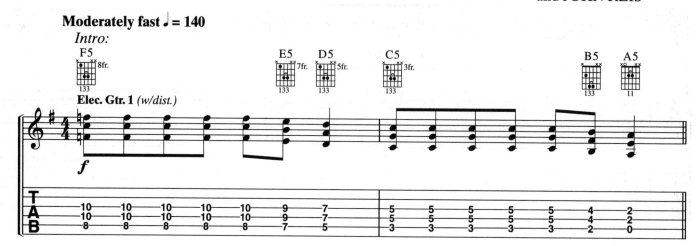

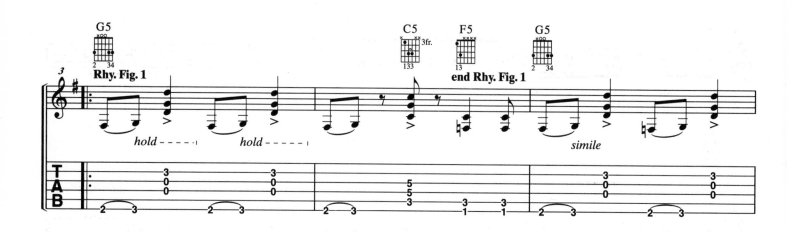

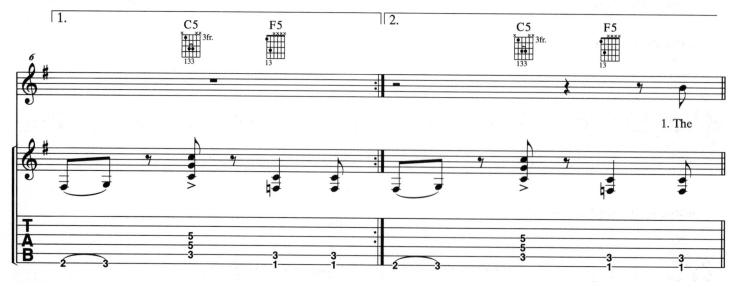

Rock Problems - 6 - 1

96

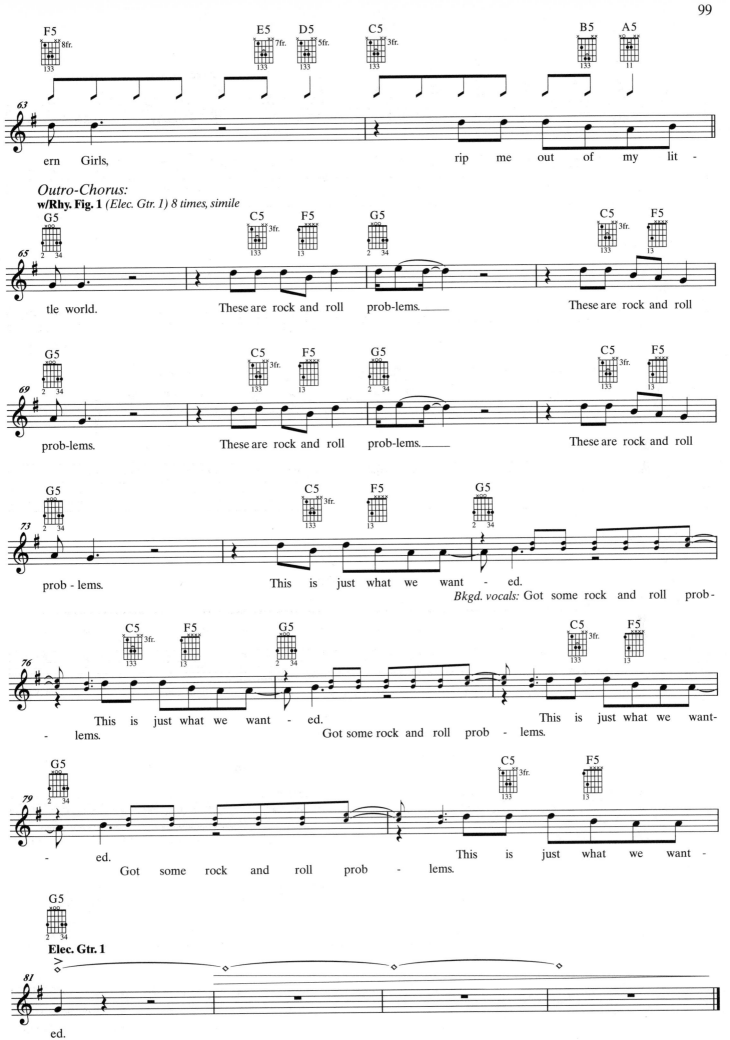

NO HURRY

Words and Music by
JAMES OTTO, BROWN ZAC
and WYATT DURRETTE

*Recording sounds one and one half steps higher than written.
Chord frames and TAB numbers relative to capo.

Verses 1 & 2:

Acous. Gtr. 2 cont. rhy. simile
Acous. Gtr. 1 tacet

my old car needs wash - ing____ and front the yard needs a trim.____ And the
(2.) wrong with an old cane fish - ing pole and the smell of ear - ly spring.__ Sit down

tel - e - phone____ keeps ring - ing,____ and the boss man knows I know it's him. And the
in a fold up eas - y chair on a qui - et shad - y riv - er bank. Let the

No Hurry - 5 - 1

RHYTHM OF LOVE

Ukulele Chord Frames

Words and Music by
TIM LOPEZ

*Acous. Gtr. 1 sounds two whole steps higher than written. TAB numbers are relative to capo position.
Acous. Gtr. 2 sounds four whole steps higher than written. TAB numbers are relative to capo position.

My head is stuck in the clouds. She begs me__ to come down, says, "Boy, quit fool - in' a-round."__

__ I told her, "I love the view__ from up here, warm sun and wind in my ear. We'll

watch the world_____ from a-bove__ as it turns__ to the rhy-thm of_____ love." We may

Rhythm of Love - 7 - 1

℅ Chorus:

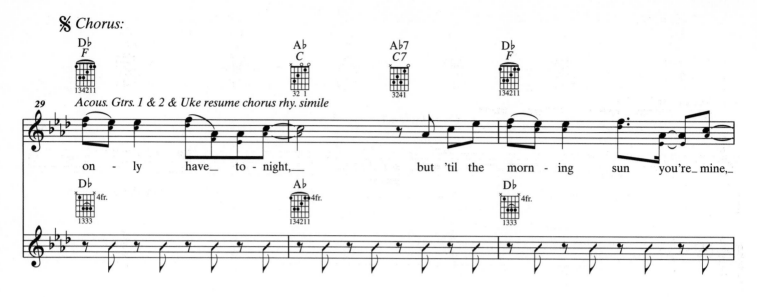

on - ly have_ to - night,___ but 'til the morn - ing sun you're_ mine,_

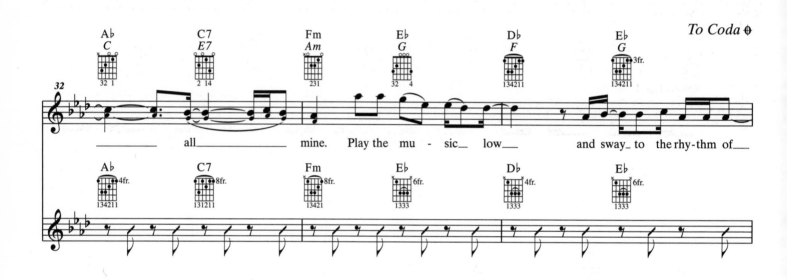

To Coda ⊕

_____ all_____ mine. Play the mu - sic_ low__ and sway_ to the rhy-thm of_

__ love.

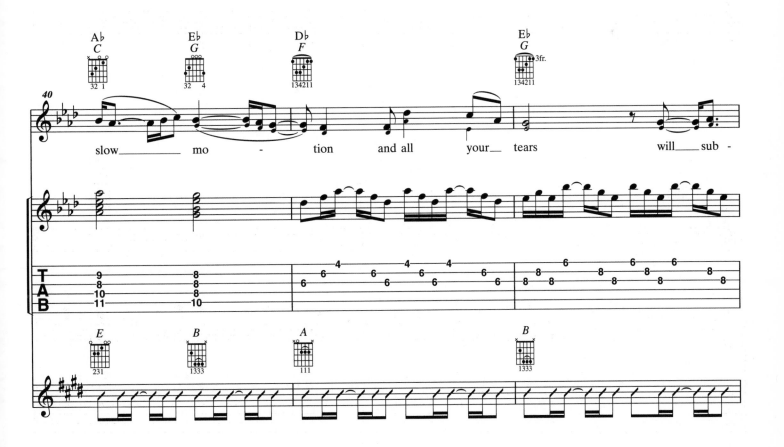

SICK OF YOU

Words and Music by
JOHN McCREA, VINCENT DIFIORE,
XAN McCURDY and GABRIEL NELSON

*Bass Gtr. pedals E throughout.

*Elec. Gtr. 1 tacet 1st 4 meas., 2nd time.

1. I'm so sick of you___ so sick of me,___ I don't_ want to be with you.
2. I'm so sick of work,___ so sick of play,___ I don't_ need an-oth-er day.

Sick of You - 5 - 1

Sick of You - 5 - 4

TEENAGE DREAM

Words and Music by
KATY PERRY, LUKASZ GOTTWALD,
MAX MARTIN, BEN LEVIN and BONNIE McKEE

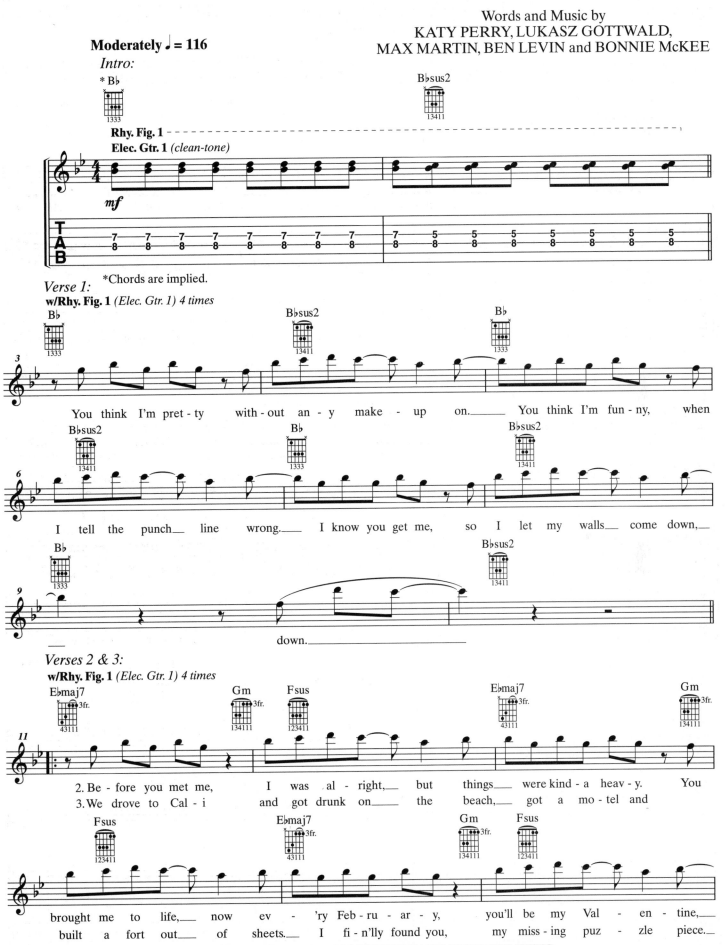

Teenage Dream - 3 - 1

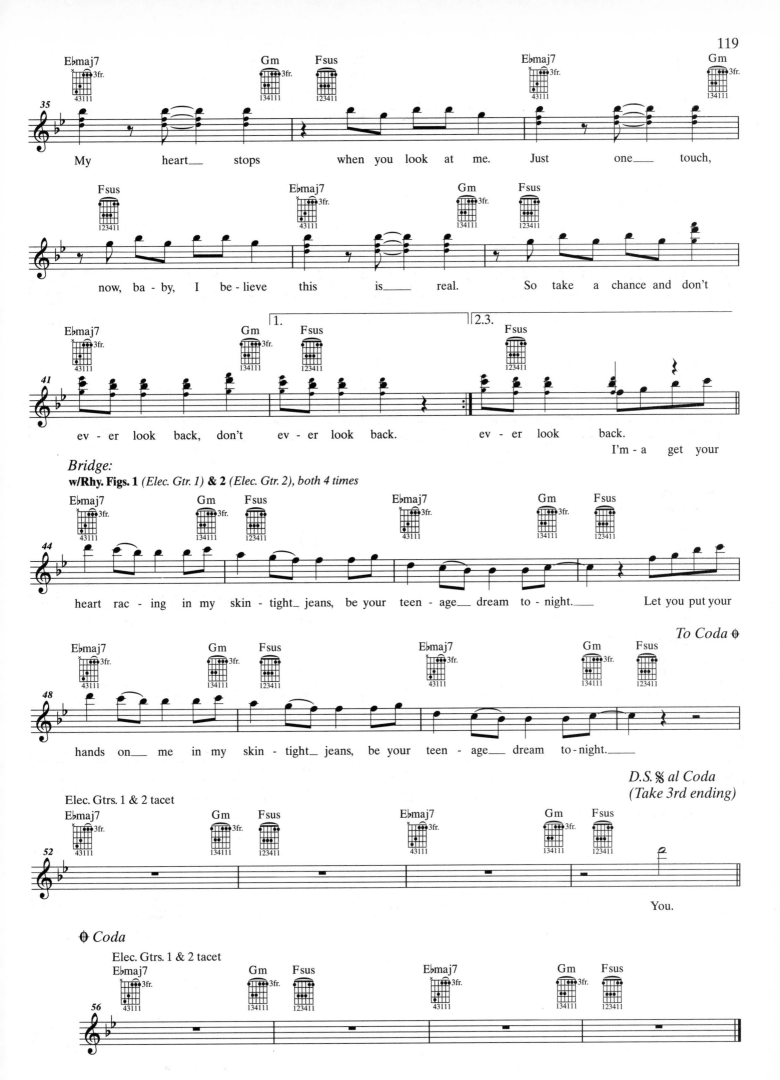

THIS TOO SHALL PASS

Words and Music by
DAMIAN JOSEPH KULASH, JR.
and TIMOTHY NORDWIND

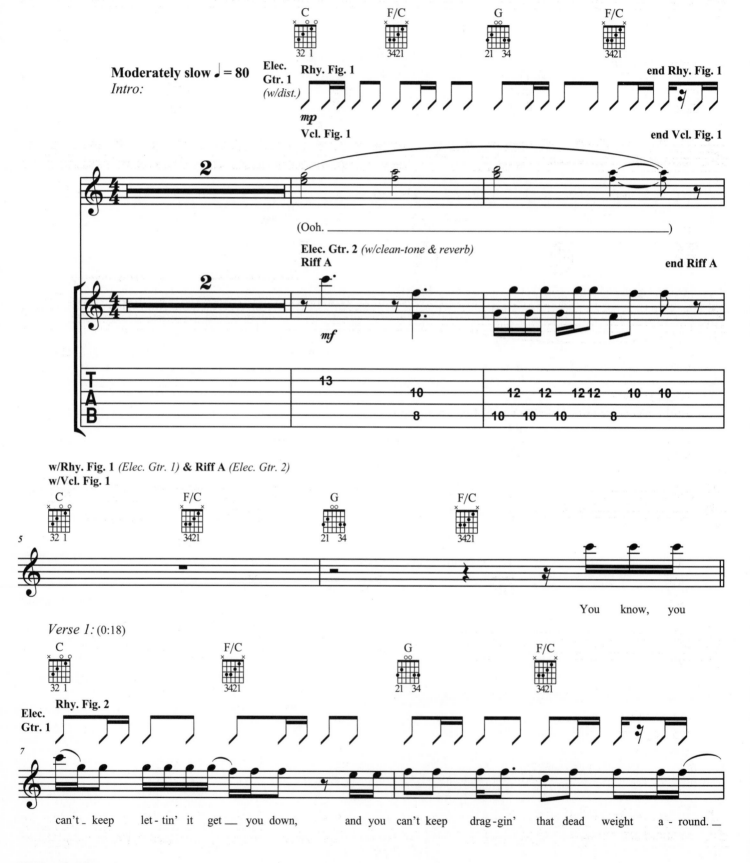

This Too Shall Pass - 6 - 1

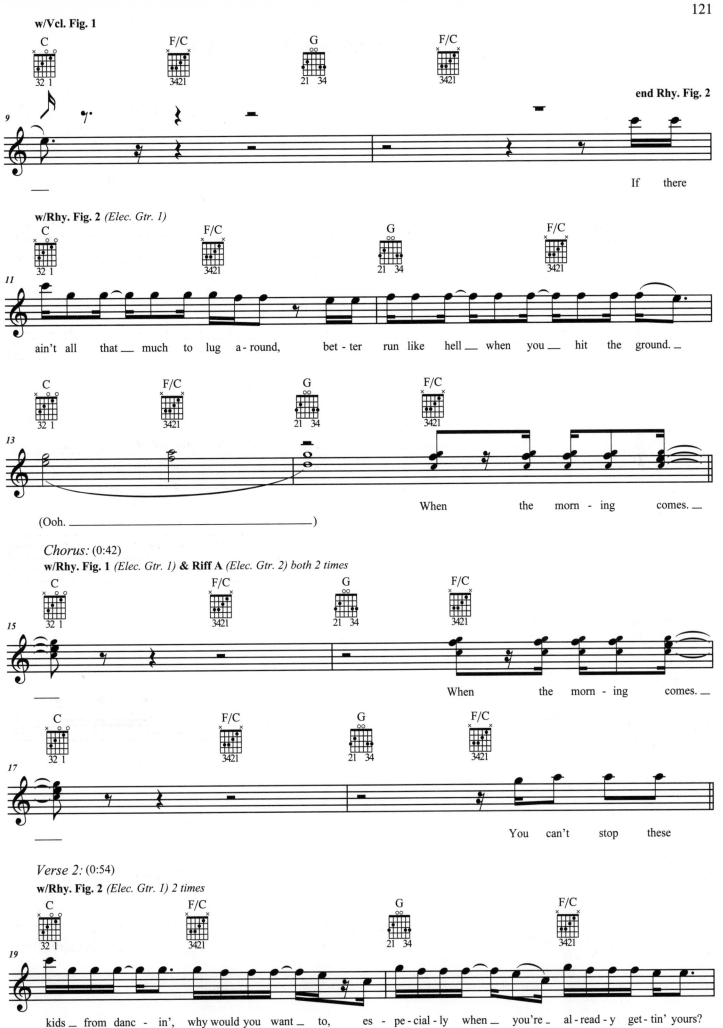

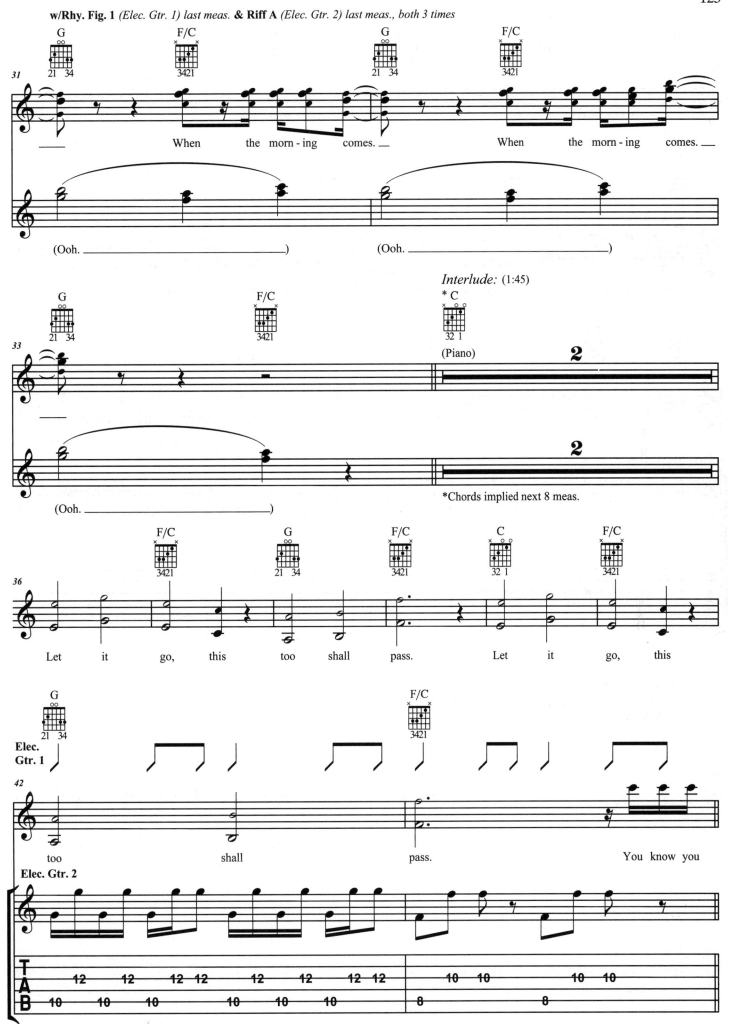

Outro: (2:15)

w/Vcl. Fig. 2 *2 times*

can't _ keep let-tin' it get _ you down. No, you can't _ keep let-tin' it get _ you down.

Yeah! If there

w/Rhy. Fig. 3 *(Elec. Gtr. 1)* **& Riff B** *(Elec. Gtr. 2)*

ain't all that _ much to lug a-round, no you can't _ keep let-tin' it get _ you down.

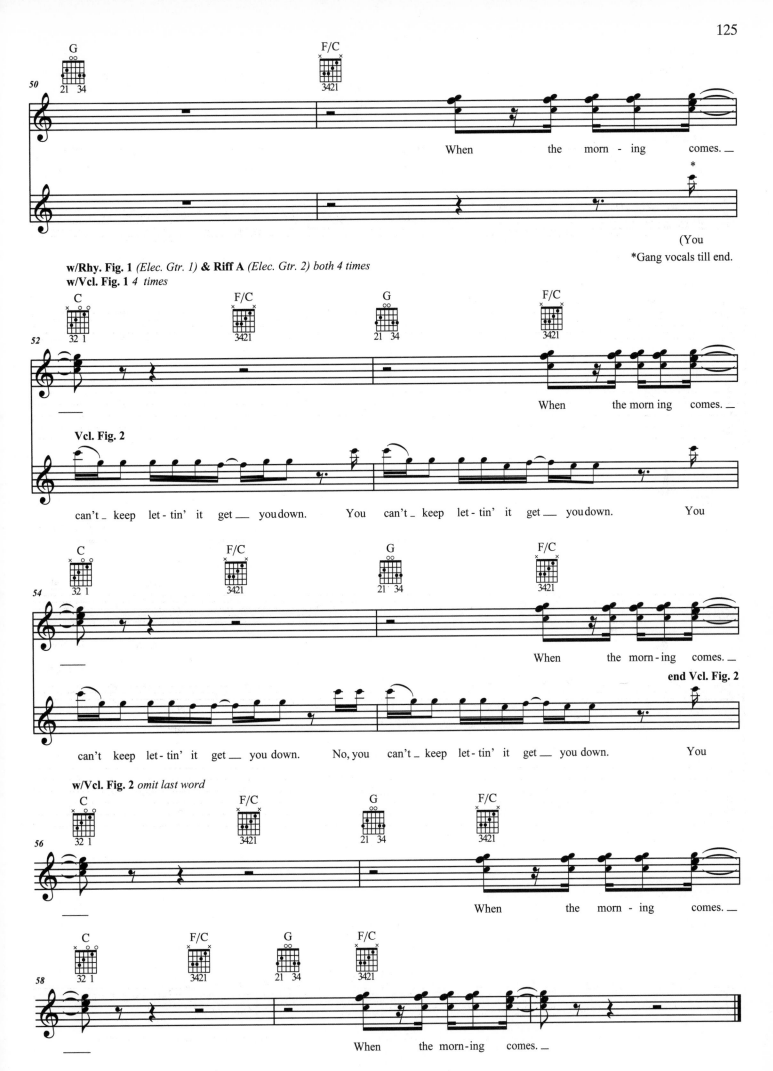

TOES

*To match recording, tune down 1/2 step:

⑥ = E♭   ③ = G♭
⑤ = A♭   ② = B♭
④ = D♭   ① = E♭

Words and Music by
SHAWN MULLINS, ZAC BROWN,
WYATT DURRETTE and JOHN HOPKINS

Moderately fast ♩ = 136

Intro:

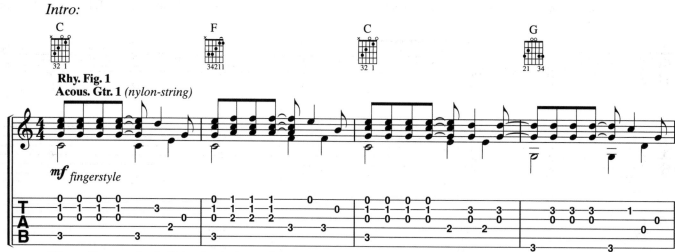

*Recording sounds a half step lower than written.

I've got my toes in the wa- ter, ass_ in the sand,_ not a wor-

Toes - 8 - 1

Pre-chorus:

Acous. Gtr. 1 cont. simile
Acous. Gtr. 2 cont. verse fills simile

Elec. Gtr.

hold throughout

But the plane brought me far-ther, I'm sur-round-ed by wa-ter, and I'm___
And co-co-nut re-plac-es the smell___ of the bar, and I don't___

___ not go-in'___ back a-gain.___
___ know if it's her___ or the rum.___ I got my

toes in the wa-ter, ass___ in the sand,___ not a wor-ry in the world,___ a cold

beer in my hand.___ Life is good___ to-day, life is good___ to-day.

A-di-os and va-ya con

Acous. Gtr. 1

Acous. Gtrs. 1 & 2, & Elec. Gtr.

Acous. Gtrs. 1 & 2 cont. in slashes

Toes - 8 - 4

Chorus:

UPRISING

Gtr. in Drop D:
⑥ = D   ③ = G
⑤ = A   ② = B
④ = D   ① = E

Words and Music by
MATTHEW BELLAMY

Moderately ♩ = 127 (♫ = ♪♪)

Intro:

*Dm

Bass *(arr. for gtr.)*

*Implied harmony.

Uprising - 6 - 1

*Elec. Gtr. plays ocatves on repeat only.

Lyrics:

green_ belts wrapped a - round our_ minds,_ and end - less _ red tape to keep the
their_ time's com - ing to an_ end,_ we have to u - ni - fy and watch our

truth con - fined.___
flag a - scend.___

%- Chorus:

They will not force___ us,

*Cue-size vocal harmonies sung on repeat only.

Cont. rhy. simile

they will stop de - grad - ing___ us.

WAKE UP EVERYBODY

Words and Music by
GENE McFADDEN, JOHN WHITEHEAD
and VICTOR CARSTARPHEN

© 1975 (Renewed) WARNER-TAMERLANE PUBLISHING CORP.
All Rights Reserved

Rap:
It's the God hour,
The morning, I wake up.
Just for the breath of life, I thank my Maker.
My mom say I come from hustlers and shakers.
My mom built it on skyscrapers and acres.
He said, take us back to where we belong.
I try to write a song as sweet as the Psalms,
Though I'm the type to bear arms
And wear my heart on my sleeve.
Even when I fail, in God I believe.
Read the days that weave through the maze
And the seasons so amazing.
Feed them and raise them,
Seasons are aging.
Earthquakes, wars, and rumors.
I want us to get by, but
We more than consumers,
We more than shooters, more than looters.
Created in this image so God live through us.
And even in this generation, living through computers,
Only love, love, love can reboot us.
(To Bridge:)